Single Mothers
are for Grown Men, ONLY!

Derrick Jaxn

Printed in the United States of America

First Printing, 2017

ISBN: 978-0-9910336-6-9

Shop Derrick Jaxn LLC

www.shopderrickjaxn.com

Table of Contents

INTRODUCTION..1

CHAPTER 1: "Single moms are poor decision makers." 13

CHAPTER 2: Single. Mother. Two Different Departments...19

CHAPTER 3: Single Mothers. Super Heroes.
No Difference..23

CHAPTER 4: The Unsung Villain...27

CHAPTER 5: For the Single Moms Who Do Date
"Thugs", Why?...33

CHAPTER 6: "But I Told You I Wasn't Ready."....................37

CHAPTER 7: "Most criminals are raised by
single mothers." 41

CHAPTER 8: "A woman can't raise a boy into a man." 47

CHAPTER 9: "Single mothers are only looking for help." 53

CHAPTER 10: "She'll always belong to her baby daddy." 57

CHAPTER 11: "Single mothers are promiscuous.".................61

CHAPTER 12: "They just want child support to spend
it on themselves." 67

CHAPTER 13: "I don't even ask him for child support." 75

CHAPTER 14: "Single mothers will never have time
to date you."...77

CHAPTER 15: "Single moms should stick to dating
single dads." 81

CHAPTER 16: "You need to be married before making children." 85

CHAPTER 17: The Hypocrisy of "Harsh Truths" Single Mothers are Told 91

CHAPTER 18: For Guys Who Refuse to Raise Another Man's Child 95

CHASE 19: Why Single Mothers are for Grown Men 99

CHAPTER 20: The REAL "Harsh Truth" About Single Motherhood 105

CHAPTER 21: Single Mother "To Not Do" List 109

CHAPTER 22: How to Know Who You're Dealing With 117

CHAPTER 23: Please Be Selfish 123

CHAPTER 24: So, What Now? 127

Introduction

Single Father.

What comes to mind when you read that? Admiration? Nobility? Self-sacrifice? Maturity? Hero?

If that's true for you, then awesome. You and I are on the same page. If you're a single father, you're likely giving so much more of yourself than you would if you had help from the mother of your child. Surely, you must make so many sacrifices on a day-to-day basis that few could conceive, much less appreciate. Hospital visits, scaling back financially, being Santa, the Tooth Fairy, doctor, and a bodyguard all in one. Life would be so much less stressful if you were to defer your responsibilities to someone else or just half step on them, but instead, I'm willing to bet you'd rather die than see your child go without. You take the emotional toll of having less help than you ask for while always giving more of yourself than you knew you had to give, with no thanks in return. But I'm thankful for you, and your child will be, too, once he or she is old enough to understand. Keep going, I'm rooting for you.

Now, let's try this again.

Single Mother.

Did anything change when you read that?

Hopefully, not, but according to many people, social media comment sections, search engines, viral videos, and mainstream media, yes. A lot changes. "Dating a single mother is like playing someone else's saved game," said one largely cosigned sentiment in a comment section under a post I saw praising single mothers. Even though a single mom is just as, if not even more so heroic than a single father, which I will explain why I believe that later, reducing her to a saved video game is a perception that apparently many agree with. As cringe-worthy as that statement is, other expressions of the like don't trail far behind any mention of the topic. It's nothing short of hate speech, but allegedly well-intentioned men and women tend to infect the dialogue with it every time I've seen single motherhood mentioned, showing a more severe diagnosis of themselves than anything. But where did it all come from?

Why is it that the term "Single Father" is a term of endearment while "Single Mother" is treated as a scarlet letter? Why is it that the parent who did not run out on their responsibility is the one society indicts? Why is it that the woman who underwent the physical pain of nine months of pregnancy, hours of labor, changes to her body, roller coaster of emotions including a possible battle with post-partum depression is the parent with the target on her back? Normalized vitriol didn't just manifest out of thin air, but it's managed to stick around unflinchingly, even when it is opposed by those with firsthand accounts both as the products of, or current heads of single-mother households.

As a social media influencer, I have a firm finger on the pulse of society's conversation around every hot-button topic from politics, to religion, celebrity scandal, social injustice; you name it. I can just about predict the flow of the majority's thought with them all; politics will turn into a reality show that will be more about the best punch line on debate night rather than who presented the best policy. Celebrity scandals are more like auditions for a new TV show and sales pitch for more social media followers because that's what comes of "break babies" or offensive speech on someone's live chat that they later "apologize" for. But when it came to the subject of single motherhood, I was way off, particularly as it pertains to dating. Growing up in a single-parent household, I saw my mother display the type of strength you hear tall tales about while equipping my four siblings and me to go out into the world and be the productive citizens we grew into with our own respective families. None of us have been to jail, strung out on drugs, or dropped out of high school like the stigmas attached to what I thought was only reserved for the worst of single mothers. If nothing else, I would think my mom and others like her would be considered the "good" ones, and from what I saw growing up, the good ones were all around while the rest were sprinkled here and there, mostly on the news and exaggerated characters in movies.

However, tens of thousands of comments from people all over the world on some of my most viral videos about single mothers taught me that my understanding did not represent what most think. According to the vocal majority, single mothers are defined by the actions of the one who left them with the sole parental responsibility regardless of the reason, which in turn, meant they're not to be romantically desired, loved, or committed to.

Self-proclaimed "good men" and women who elected themselves to speak on behalf of the so-called good men they thought they knew volunteered ignorance from every direction about how single mothers deserved the absolute least from the dating scene. No, not just the "bad" ones, but all of them, or for the ones with vain attempts to be unbiased, "most" single mothers. The blanket that covered a woman who was forced to do her best to supplement for a second parent when it's already hard enough being one, was so filled with filthy and disgusting generalizations you'd wonder if the problem people had with them was personal.

However, I'm usually not too emotionally attached one way or the other when it comes to the responses to my posts. Years of seeing hate speech from anonymous troll accounts and my insatiable cravings for healthy debate numb me to those thoughts expressed whether they agree with me or not. I do, however, moderate when needed to keep the conversation productive, but I prefer to let all perspectives be considered.

But on one particular video I uploaded, titled *Single Mothers are for Grown Men...ONLY!,* the conversation was far past what any moderation could fix. It was completely shattered into pieces. Not due to vulgarities or bickering between the commenters, but rather because of the harmonized fallacies in the objectifications to my stance that it takes a certain level of maturity to be able to truly appreciate a single mother, particularly when it came to dating her. Simple enough, right?

Apparently not. Misdirected blame and unfounded malice surfaced quicker than you could blink, and repeatedly so with every related video on the topic afterwards. That's when I realized that this is much bigger than just a social media post or online conversation; this is the condition of our culture.

Where there's smoke, there's fire, and some of the common threads were billowing with thick, suffocating smog.

Among the pollution were firsthand accounts from single mothers who'd heard hurtful outside opinions like those expressed in the comment section before, and the effect it had on their faith in both love and humanity. Accounts of staying completely off the dating scene for frustration of getting hopes up and subsequently let down when the only agenda was sexual. One woman even stated she was, "done defending her character even if it meant dying alone." I can only imagine what it must feel like to equate the simple act of dating to a war where you're constantly defending yourself, and then being so exhausted that in order to simply not have to fight, you also have to surrender your hope of being loved. That penetrated the emotionless shell I had developed, and motivated me to take this conversation to a new level, to fix it once and for all.

Is it ambitious, possibly too ambitious to think that I can? Maybe. I'm aware that I'm no household name nor do I have a TV show or anything that would just give me the power to speak to an entire culture that's been misled. But, I also realize that one person can spark the change needed, and if I can just do that, then I will have done my job.

Again, this goes beyond a video or comment rebuttal. This is a malfunction in the common-sense department of an entire society. This is not only a step in the wrong direction; it's a slip 'n slide of unhealthy viewpoints that lead to a pool of continued stereotypes, abuse, and misery for the undeserving. For many, aspirations of being loved properly, fully, and faithfully are hanging in the balance. Both men and women need the perspective adjustment so we can stop passing down these misperceptions that cause us to raise Internet and real-life trolls, who grow up to call themselves adults. Even worse than those trolls are the dating prospects that meet single mothers and pose as grown men when really, they're mental adolescents at best. These males can pass off the byproduct of their own lack of integrity as ramifications of single mothers' choices while continuing to seek out other women to leave in the same situation later.

It's important to note that throughout this book, I will be referencing single mothers as a group. However, I'm not speaking to the entire group. I'm speaking to what I've seen and truly believe represents the majority, but I'm aware that there is a sub group who, while under promoted, does exist.

Leave it to the media that both in "reality" TV and scripted programs, single mothers are depicted as nothing more than this sub group, just like every other marginalized community who gets painted by a broad brush by the actions of a few. Whether it's Muslims who get associated with a select few terrorists, African Americans who get associated with inner city crime rates, or foreigners who get associated with illegal immigrants, the justification of mistreatment and misrepresentation starts with a smear campaign focused on a small portion of a larger population. Single mothers are no different.

The news repeatedly shows statistics of the shortcomings of children raised by them; box office movie roles portray them as drug addicts, and even on social media, if a video is going viral, it's rarely showing them in a positive light. It's not that these don't reflect any part of reality, it's just that a disproportionate amount of focus tells a false story that all, or even a majority of single mothers, live these lives when that's not the case. If you look around, you'll see teachers, counselors, authors, business owners, and just everyday women who will never make the news or land a starring role in a TV series because they are just normal people, and the same goes for single mothers. Their underrepresentation makes it easy for the world to forget that they even exist, making the negative exception seem like the rule.

Anytime I've defended single mothers from the onslaught of these negative generalizations by highlighting those who represent the best among them, I can count on dozens of people proclaiming, "Not all single mothers are like that." In the interest of fairness, I agree. Single mothers are not monolithic one way or the other. They come in different shapes, sizes, backgrounds, experiences, stages of life, and mistakes they're still making. Some of them are indeed the drama kept up in the father of the child's new relationships. Some are vindictive, spiteful, and self-proclaimed "petty". Some teach their toddler to twerk to go viral online and leave their children with just anyone. I've always made the distinction between these women as "Baby Mamas" as opposed to the esteemed title of a single mother. I would be doing single mothers an injustice by lumping them all together when their actions make them incontestably different, yet society doesn't see it that way.

Society looks at "Baby Mamas" no different from the real single mothers who cry themselves to sleep at night, not because they're lonely, but because they know their child deserves two parents but they're only capable of being one, or the mothers who see their child's father spending money on random women while she's struggling to pay for daycare. Those who go to church with their children trying to steer them the right way, but have to endure hypocritical stares from all of the holier-than-thou's because she had children out of wedlock and is forced to take care of them on her own. Those women who ignore their own hunger pangs so their children will never know the feeling. In the eyes and treatment of society, there's no difference between them and "Baby Mamas", which is where a major problem lies.

Just because I'm not chiming in with the large part of society's slander against single mothers doesn't mean I'm not objective enough to see that in the same way a "Deadbeat Dad" is not the same as a single father. There is also a difference between the majority of single mothers who hold down the fort and those "Baby Mamas" who leave the fort in flames. For the sake of effective dialogue, we shouldn't generalize all mothers who are single one way or the other, and neither will I. For the sake of this book, I want to make it clear my views on single mothers are not a one-size-fits-all, and neither are the views of a man any woman would benefit from being romantically involved with.

So, I'm not here to take eligible bachelors through psychological puberty in hopes that they stop missing out on what could be special due to generalizations because that woman has a child. What I am here to do is prove why what some men believe to be justifiable reasons to romantically avoid single mothers or treat them as less than says more about them than it does any woman they think would want them in the first place. What I'm going to share represents the perspectives of the covertly present group of grown men who step in and step up to the plate and are glad they did so. The forthcoming truths will already be engrained in the minds of those men who, even if they're not currently in the role of a stepfather, wouldn't let the possibility of being one cost them the opportunity to be with a phenomenal woman. This group of men, like many good men, tends not to represent the vocal majority, so I'm giving them a megaphone to counterbalance the deceit that "No man would date a single mom," as proclaimed by those who currently dominate the conversation. The truth is, little boys would never date a single mom, and that's fine, because single mothers are for grown men only.

CHAPTER 1

"Single moms are poor decision makers."

When I was a pre-teen, I remember a game I used to play with my crush where we wrote down our dream car, house, and honeymoon vacation destination we'd have ten years from then. The goal was pretty much to out-extravagant each other. Lamborghinis, ten bedroom mansions, and Bermudas were all over the paper. You'd think we had actually seen any of this in real life, but we hadn't. We just looked optimistically into the future and craved the best for ourselves, as I imagine did everyone else.

But, we grew up, and not only were we not each other's crushes anymore, we didn't quite come into that lavish lifestyle as we'd planned. She got a job at a local restaurant bussing tables because the job she'd gone to school for didn't pay enough to where she would be willing to relocate so far away from her family. I moved into a 900-square-foot house in North Carolina so that I could handle my school loan payments, and drove my company car for both work and hanging out on the weekend when I could afford to splurge on the parking fees.

I think I speak for us both when I say, it's not exactly the future we'd planned for ourselves, but it could've been worse. We weren't the only ones who had to adjust our timing of our goals to roll with life's punches, and just because things didn't happen exactly how we mapped them out didn't mean we didn't deserve to be happy. Our situations were due to us living life like most young adults; instead of launching multi-million dollar businesses that would've guaranteed us massive success, we got into school sports, SGA, went on movie dates, and to concerts. Some people were lucky enough to do the same thing and strike gold, but we struck reality with a chance to still have gold as wiser, smarter adults going forward.

When we look at single mothers, they're similar. They're the ones who can admit that maybe they haven't struck gold, but they're not out of the game either. They're blamed for making poor decisions when a more accurate summation would be that they made risky decisions common to almost all of us--having sex with someone who's not guaranteed to stay.

I first saw the assertion that single mothers were poor decision makers from a male YouTuber, although that wouldn't be the last. I'll bet anything that it's not what the rappers he listens to makes songs about, yet he doesn't eviscerate them about "poor decision" making. If his boys bragged to him about smashing a sexy girl on the first night and never calling her again, do you think he'd clutch his pearls and gasp at how horrible their decision making was then? If he's anything like a majority of men today, probably not. The porn industry grosses billions of dollars every year, doing the very thing he casts aspersions on women with children for doing, yet that doesn't draw such criticism. So why is it that when a woman has sex with someone, be it a complete stranger, long-time boyfriend, or her husband, and she's left alone, that's a reflection of her ability to make a sound decision?

By that definition, our standard of a choice that's "smart" would be more like a premonition. She would have to have been able to see into the future and know that the man she was having sex with would leave at the mere fear that he could be the father. Either that, or we believe a woman should expect that by default, men will not handle their responsibilities. However, if a woman did believe that, she would be labeled as "bitter" and "scorned", labels that already plague single mothers.

Her guard would be seen as a knock against her that she doesn't see a man for his potential and holds on to her past. The only "men" this would work out well for would be men who never wanted to be held to the standard of being a man in the first place. Why? Because if you're never expected to do right, it won't be counted as your fault when you do wrong. It becomes more of a responsibility of the person who was wronged to know that who she was dealing with would do her wrong, instead of the one who did her wrong to simply not be an asshole.

For conversation's sake, let's just say this male YouTuber wasn't talking about simply having sex when he referenced the poor decision single mothers were guilty of making, whether protected or unprotected, because he understands that no matter what, all sex runs the risk of pregnancy happening, and surely he's taken time to consider that. Maybe he was referring to the actual act of getting pregnant.

Well, news flash, women don't go down into their ovaries and flip the "pregnant" switch. It's not some multiple choice question they get asked by their uterus. They take the risk with a man who also takes the risk, and single mothers stick it out if things don't go exactly how they planned. There's nothing irresponsible about stepping up to the plate even though you're not exactly ready for the pitch. What's irresponsible is staying in the dugout when it's your turn to bat.

Even if the man does remain active in the child's life but is not with the mother romantically, blame should not, by default, be placed with the woman. However, if 100% of the blame actually is on the woman, and it was solely her choice to end that relationship, she's still not wrong for doing so, and the same applies to a man and vice versa. We're growing, evolving beings. Two people who were great for each other in a particular season of their lives may be better off finding love elsewhere after some time has passed and changes have taken place. The thing is, you can break up with and move on from a relationship partner, but that child is yours no matter what. So it's unreasonable to hold someone, anyone, accountable for their relationship status after their parental status has changed when the two are completely separate.

But for conversation's sake, let's say he wasn't slandering single mothers for merely having sex, nor for getting pregnant, because he knows he'd sound absolutely absurd and quite shallow in his thinking. Let's give him even more benefit of the doubt, that he must've been alluding to her poor decision making of not exploring reactive measures, such as an abortion.

While reasons for abortions and feelings about them may vary, one thing's for sure, he clearly wouldn't be pro choice in this situation because pro choice is defined as tolerance for whatever choice a woman makes with her pregnancy, in which shaming her for not making a decision of his liking would conflict with that. But then again, he also wouldn't be pro life because, well, pro life means being in favor of a woman not having an abortion. So the only option left is that he must be pro "go back in time and do it all over again." Insert sarcasm.

So what is it, then, that equates to being such a poor decision maker and warrants the negativity that single moms receive? If her decision to have sex is one shared with nine out of ten of adults, that can't be why she's singled out. If she can't biologically choose to get pregnant, that can't be it either. There is no time machine, to my knowledge, that we can hop in and undo all of the things that didn't work out in our life. So what is this decision-making sin that single moms are so guilty of? Being single?

CHAPTER 2

Single. Mother. Two Different Departments.

Let's start with the fact that it's already hard for anyone, especially a woman, to find a qualified love interest these days. The games people play, the masks people wear over their true colors, and the long-term effects of trusting the wrong one are enough to slow anyone down on their pursuit of love. Add a child into the mix and the stakes get higher as well, and the tolerance for B.S. becomes non-existent.

However, the story of a mother who's single isn't always so black and white. There are several reasons one could be single, but even if you looked at what you felt was the absolute most deplorable and unacceptable one, the parental and relationship status has no relationship as it pertains to her character.

Most people can think of at least one father who leaves much to be desired as a relationship partner, but when it comes to his children, it's a completely different story. He's there for them, provides for them, teaches and engages with them regularly, etc. However, as a partner, he was the biggest cheater the world had ever seen. Why is it that even with this familiar reality, we still can't detach a mother from her role or status as a relationship partner?

We count it as a strike if she's not in a relationship, regardless of the reason, yet we give men passes for being adulterers so long as he's "good to his kids, though." Honestly, you could make the case that not being a great relationship partner taints his example-setting value, but that's not the point. The point is, if he can get a pass for actually being at fault for why a relationship ended, why is it that women aren't afforded the same leniency, even if why the relationship ended wasn't her fault? Or maybe it was her fault, and it was still for the best.

Scenario: Woman meets man. Woman falls in love with man. Woman and man want to have sex, like normal couples in a relationship, so they do. Woman gets pregnant, and man now has to actually face the reality that he's going to be linked to this woman for the rest of his life in some way. The moment this happens, he subconsciously blames her for getting pregnant as if she took his penis off of his pelvis and penetrated herself, and treats her with the malice he now holds in his heart for her, although she's actually done nothing to deserve it. She's not in a hurry to leave because not too long ago, things were just fine, but he continues to make the relationship difficult to the point it's unbearable, oftentimes with blatant disrespect and infidelity.

Somewhere around the time the baby is born, she decides that she needs to separate from him because she can't afford to be in an unhealthy relationship any longer now that her child is born. She needs to be the best version of herself so she can give her child the best version of herself. He takes that as a "get out of parenthood free pass" and goes ghost on both of them, justifying his neglect to his child because it was the mother's decision to be done with him, when subconsciously, he just wasn't ready to face the fact that he's a father now.

We are living in a society that says the mother is wrong for making that decision, and with that, it's time to relocate to Planet Common Sense where we understand that she's not, nor does it have any bearing on her as a woman. While the bigger point is that her relationship status altogether is completely unrelated to her as a mother, I would at least hope that we could gateway from A to Z by getting to point B, where we don't say by default, 'single' plus 'mother' equals a "bad person deserving of bashing". Although it would still be logically flawed, I could make sense of someone saying that if a woman began to create an unhealthy relationship environment, that must mean she's a bad parent, too. But as we know with the example of how society regards men who actually do this often, we're capable of seeing the truth, we're just choosing to be blind.

A single woman, for any reason, can still be fully capable of raising her child to be a productive and healthy citizen as well as be an asset to any man as a relationship partner. Whatever happened that caused her previous relationship to end not only does not define her, it would be determined by a completely different set of characteristics than what it would take to raise a child.

To be a good relationship partner with another adult, a woman is expected to grow with him, co-pilot, and romantically put forth consistent effort to satisfy him while rightfully expecting the same in return. As a parent, her job is to raise a completely dependent individual, be the authority, and maintain a healthy balance between nurturer and disciplinarian.

Although those characteristics have distinct differences, could it be that the reason why so many men group them together is because some men have the same expectations of their woman that a child would have of his or her mother? That's another subject, but judging by the immature thought pattern of those who try to defend their assertions of a mother's singleness as a direct reflection of her value as a relationship partner, parent, or woman, it's not far-fetched.

CHAPTER 3

Single Mothers. Super Heroes. No Difference.

I mentioned earlier that I believe single parents to be heroic, but moreso, a single mother, and this is why. A single father has to deal with many of the same obstacles a single mother does as far as carrying the sole financial and parental responsibility for a child, but as a man, the world is a bit less cold to him. In fact, he may get a few freebies for being a single father whereas a mother would have to trade that in for "should've known better" stares, snickers, and ridicule.

So, when compared to super heroes, there's not much separation at all besides the part where the single mothers are non-fictional. I mean, a super hero can usually fly, but being able to wake her children up, get them dressed, get herself dressed, make breakfast, force them to eat, get them to school, and make it to work on time enough mornings to keep her job is practically the same thing. Super heroes are also known to have super strength, but imagine having to bear the pressure of being a parent before you probably were ready to, having every decision's outcome for your child, whether good or bad, fall solely on you, be judged by society, misrepresented in the media, depended on fully by another human when you yourself would like to have someone to depend on, putting yourself last so that your child never goes without, and still fight unequal treatment as a woman on a daily basis. If that's not super human strength, I don't know what is.

The courage of a super hero to face evil in order to save the world pales in comparison to the courage it takes to face a two-person job as only one for the next eighteen years, but that distinction is closest shared with a single mother. Alternatively, some women may even find themselves putting up with a toxic relationship much longer than they would normally, due to this fear. They have to pick a "poison" of being stranded or being damaged and unfortunately, choose the latter, but many single mothers are women who chose to face that fear despite the stigma that came along with it. Even for the sake of family, it benefits no party involved to remain in an unhealthy relationship, although societal pressure would lead us to believe otherwise. An absentee father is better than an abusive one. A lack of help is better than help doing badly. Having to be strong by force is better than suffering by choice. When a woman steps out and chooses to face judgment, backlash, a lack of resources, heightened stress and responsibility for her child's well-being, as opposed to a life of companionship at the cost of her mental and sometimes physical health, it's worth being commended.

Most distinctly, in the same way that super heroes are treated as though they are villains, so is a single mother. She plays one of the most selfless roles in the world, takes on full-time job-like demands, and doesn't get her proper credit by anyone besides the person she's doing it all for, her child, which usually happens once a year on Mother's Day and when that child reaches adulthood. If she does air out her grievances for mere moral support, it is instead met with self-respectability lectures, yet if she doesn't, she's left to suffer in silence and bite her tongue when she's still met with unsolicited advice by people who don't know the half of what she's dealing with.

One of the few differences between single moms and super heroes is that opposed to some botched science experiment or getting bit by a spider, her powers are obtained by experience, a lack of options, and a lot of faith. Another difference is that unlike some of our favorite super heroes, she doesn't have healing powers that allow her wounds to heal in a matter of seconds mid-battle. In fact, her wounds take quite a bit of time to heal because the harder you try, the worse things hurt, and that's if she's able to heal at all. That's why we have to keep in mind that as comical as some of the beliefs surrounding single motherhood are, this is no comic book. This is real life.

CHAPTER 4

The Unsung Villain

The most convenient assertion to make about a woman who has a child by a man who turns out to be an absentee father is that she should've known better. However, it's also the most unrealistic and unfair expectation of a woman to hold her responsible for future actions of someone based on the facade that person shows up front.

There's no amount of criminal background checking, report building, or palm reading that can tell you whether or not a man will choose to run out on his responsibility as a father. There are some men who were raised in two-parent households, hold steady jobs, whatever else you think should qualify him as a wholesome person, and when they find out they're going to be father, they run out the same way the stereotypical "thug" does. The only common denominator for men who stay and raise their children is the desire to stay and raise their children, not outside "indicators" that a woman is responsible for recognizing.

As mentioned before, the person and the parent are two different compartments. While many people manage to be consistent in both whether good or bad, there are plenty who hide their discrepancy until it's too late, but only men get the pass for it. A future deadbeat dad can be the most chivalrous, kind, caring, charismatic man in the world to a woman in the beginning or even for a length of time in a serious relationship, and then turn out to be a complete monster once a child comes into the picture. It may be due to fear or simply frustration of making a child with a woman he didn't plan on having in his life for the rest of his life, but either way, the "reset" button of going missing is afforded almost exclusively to men, and without social consequence.

Even worse is the fact that oftentimes, these men will allow the worst of them to come to the forefront in the form of displaced anger as a retaliation to a woman they impregnated for being impregnated. No, she didn't fertilize herself, but in his mind, she did since he had been having sex before with no problem, but now "all of a sudden" there's a baby on the way. He was fine being a decent human being to her under the condition that he never had to face the consequences of a risk he chose to take by having sex with her, and when that changed, so did he.

He goes from some version of courting her to cold shoulders and moody conversations that escalate out of nowhere ending in him hanging up and/or not wanting to talk to her for days or even weeks. The panic of trying to shift one's entire life in preparation for parenthood becomes a burden he places solely on her and blames her for it since society vouches for the delusion that she's at fault, not the two of them. He forces a situation to where the mother is to either submit herself to such harsh treatment or distance herself from him and into single parenthood, which in her case, would only make things even more challenging.

This is just one variation of the common plight of a closet deadbeat, or what I call the Unsung Villain that many single mothers know very well. He doesn't reveal up front that he's going to be one, but through the path of denial, fear, and deferment of accountability, he lumps himself in with all the rest of absentee fathers. Closet Deadbeats deploy several strategies of both hiding their true identities before and as their damage is done.

Some will blame their deadbeat ways on a sudden skepticism of who's actually the father of their child as they apply no real effort to verify one way or the other. Others simply half-ass their involvement in their child's life to an extent where it's no longer healthy for him or her, forcing the mother to keep the child away from the father, which in turn, takes the blame off of him, so he chooses to see it. The excuses, masks, and deceitful tricks of a Closet Deadbeat are many, and it doesn't help that to the outside world, perception is reality.

Not having to be pregnant for nine months nor attached at the hip to his child only assists in the illusion that he's childless and faultless, which many are fooled by. It's easy to wag your finger at a single mother who couldn't hide it even if she did want to, but give a pass to a man who by a simple decision to, can pretend his induction into fatherhood never happened.

Some will even go on to have families later, and function as the dad they never were to their previous offspring. They feel like they can simply start over new and do it "right" this time with a woman they want to be with while escaping the feeling of being a deadbeat dad. However, it's even worse now that both his child and the child's mom can see that he had the capacity to be a father the entire time; he simply made up in his mind that his first child wasn't good enough to deserve that from him.

So where does this leave the mother? Firstly, in a position where she has to explain this to her baby without breaking his or her heart. Secondly, it makes her more vulnerable for judgment since this otherwise "great dad" doesn't take care of his child, she must be the determining factor, a narrative oftentimes promoted by absentee fathers. She's more susceptible to being seen as bitter, hateful, or jealous when really, while she would have good reason to be all three, she simply wants the help with her child she was due since she got help getting pregnant. If she asks for help, she's needy, but if she doesn't, she's stranded, and at the end of the day, very few people will truly know what she's going through because the deadbeat dad has only revealed his true self to her and their child, while still hiding that dark side of his identity from everyone else.

CHAPTER 5

For the Single Moms Who Do Date "Thugs", Why?

For those wondering, yes, there is a flip side to the unsung villain, the side where men come in black and white, no blurred lines or special effects to hide behind. They are who they are unabashedly in every area of their lives. They walk like a duck, talk like a duck, and even have duck tatted on their foreheads just so there's no confusion. So why is it that a woman would ever entertain such a man?

First, let's get it understood that the group of women who knowingly choose to date these guys does not represent the majority. "Thugs" who have nothing to hide are guys who, despite their socially unacceptable ways, do exhibit a level of transparency that's atypical of most people in general. But why is it that a woman would ever entertain such a man? Of course, she's the end decision maker, so the simple answer is that it's because she wants to.

A more thorough answer by way of feedback from hundreds of thousands of women who frequent the comment sections of my posts alluding to this topic, most admit that they date or have entertained straight up "bad boys" because they're tired of being fooled by the wolves in sheep's clothing. Again, it doesn't absolve the woman of her dating choice when it conflicts with what she says she wants, but it adds context worthy of being considered. It's not fun dealing with anyone who doesn't have your best interests at heart, but at least with one who's straight up about it, the guessing is removed. So even with your guard up when dealing with them, there's a peace of mind that what you see is what you get, which is better than being blindsided any day because that's when you get hurt the most.

It's similar to hopping in a cage with a lion. You already know to either run or be ready to dodge the lion the moment it leaps to attack you. But if you're in a pet store and hold a kitten that has the bite of a lion, you're in much more trouble. The same is true for men who come into a woman's life one way, and turn into another throughout the course of a relationship once her feelings are invested. And men can play like they're naive all they want, but they know waiting until she's emotionally in too deep is no accident. That's when she's the most vulnerable and least likely to leave, even if it's in her best interest to. However, when it comes to a woman who's dating an overt "bad boy" who's no longer hiding behind his mask, if he ever did, we act as if it's supposed to be simple to walk away, and if she doesn't, it's a direct reflection of her character.

So where does that leave us? For one, it leaves us neglecting the part where single mothers aren't blaming the "thugs" they procreated with for still being thugs, but rather for not being present in their child's life whether physically or financially, and being able to avoid the same judgment and criticism that she receives.

It also leaves us displacing the blame of a mom being left to raise a child alone on the mom and not the absentee father. We call it, "stop making excuses for single moms" when really it's the framing of mothers that's excusing the should-be fathers. In fact, it's even worse than excusing their behavior, it's ignoring it altogether, which in turn, facilitates more of the end result that society claims to be so passionate about finding a solution for.

CHAPTER 6

"But I Told You I Wasn't Ready."

The ironic thing about having any kind of fun is, you don't always think through the consequences of what that fun comes with, outside of the time of your life you'll have in the process. If you eat a slice of cheesecake, you're usually not thinking of the extra pounds that are getting ready to show on your love handles. If you take a couple of drinks, you're not thinking of the headache in the morning. When you play a game of pickup basketball for the first time in years, you're not focused on how sore you'll be in the morning. Regardless of what you didn't think of, it doesn't change the price you pay for whatever indulgence you chose. Whether you're ready to pay that price or not, you don't have a choice to run out on your tab.

However, when it comes to impregnating a woman after indulging in sex, men will hide behind, "I told you I wasn't ready," as one Facebook commenter stated she was told by her child's father. It's the luxury afforded by a man's anatomy that only one parent has to carry the child, and should she not bow down to his demands to get rid of it, or read his mind that he wanted nothing to do with parenthood despite his actions that increased his chances to 50/50, he transfers all responsibility for his decision onto her.

I even saw another commenter write, "I don't blame a man for running out on a kid he wasn't ready for." On one hand, that's a better alternative than staying in the child's life and ruining it. But more realistically, how do you not blame someone for creating a child that didn't ask to be here, then not even trying to step up to their responsibility as a parent? Women aren't always ready for the child they bring into the world either. As a matter of fact, most would admit they were everything but ready, yet there's such a thing called, "get ready" that adults do when someone else's well-being is on the line for their choices.

Let's not fool ourselves into thinking that any woman grows up with aspirations of raising a child by herself. However, it happens. But, when a man says, "I told you I wasn't ready," it's treating the mother as if the decision to get pregnant was hers. Either that, or it's saying that the decision to remain pregnant was hers which would, in turn, mean that the man had already decided on her behalf that abortion was a viable option before having sex. That means that the party whose body would be in no way affected one way or the other, decided that a procedure the woman would have to go through would be something she should consider without ever consulting with her about it. Either way you look at it, the thought is senseless and manipulative.

By that rationale, if a woman doesn't listen to what she was "told", even if what she was "told" came a day late and dollar short, does that mean she signed up for single parenthood and deserves to be left alone? Does that mean that his only responsibility after impregnating her is simply telling her whether or not he's ready? Does that mean if he's not ready, he can just opt out until he is, or disappear permanently with no accountability? No. So why do we continue to let men get away with this weak excuse while claiming to give "tough love" to single mothers in the form of unfair policing and displaced blame?

On the same token, telling women, "Don't get pregnant until you're ready," is like telling anyone, "Don't fall in love unless it's with the one you'll marry." Of course, it's well-intentioned advice, but if I may step into reality for just a moment, it doesn't always work like that. Even though we can take steps to try and reduce the chances of ending up with a broken heart from falling in love prematurely, there's no real way to finesse life perfectly in your best interests without ever taking a loss. We weren't designed that way. Instead we were designed to make mistakes and have the option to know better going forward. We were designed to see that even in our mistakes, blessings can bloom, and that at the end of the day we should make the best of it and be grateful. We were designed to have unique experiences and unapologetically be a work in progress our entire life.

The problem is, we don't give single mothers any of those options. We give them scorn for not having predicted their predicament and allow them to be written off as "damaged goods", instead of humans. We grasp the concept of, "You can't make a man stay who doesn't want to stay," when speaking generally of relationships but when a child is involved, we do a 180 and hold the woman liable for not doing the very thing we told her she could not do. As a society, we go back on every front of common sense to reinforce ignorant bias about single parents instead of simply addressing the issue head-on with the one responsible, which is the parent who left.

CHAPTER 7

"Most criminals are raised by single mothers."

One thing I love about the Internet is the abundance of knowledge available at our disposal. One thing that frustrates me about the Internet is the abundance of people who either don't use that knowledge or intentionally misuse it to mislead others.

Case in point: It's common to see the distorted fact that most criminals come from single-parent households, many of which are headed by women. Although you won't have to look any further than Fox News or peer-reviewed articles doing their best to blame their logical invalidities on the numbers, I've seen this used in online debates more than anywhere else. It's nothing less than propaganda, which is statistics that intentionally mislead by removing proper context and filling in the blank with whatever angle will support the point a person is trying to make. It's not that there aren't influential factors involved when looking at the causes of something such as a criminal, but some people cherry pick which factors were the biggest influences or make them up out of thin air.

For instance, "Black-on-black crime is a huge problem." This is true, except the distinction of "black" is an unrelated factor to the cause of the crime. Every race commits crime against those of the same race at relatively the same rate. Instead, proximity would be a better association if we're looking to identify influential factors since most crimes take place between people in the same neighborhoods. So, the real narrative should be that close proximity crime is a huge problem.

With that being said, if it's not single mothers that are the major factors in the raising of criminals, then what is it? Simple--the health of the environment the child is raised in, which is influenced by whether or not one parent is bearing the responsibilities of both, and less by the character or relationship status of said parent. Single or not, if a parent is unhealthy mentally or emotionally, he or she will create an unhealthy environment, and from that, the child would be at a disadvantage when it comes to growing up into a productive citizen. Although the same would apply to a two-parent household, if an otherwise healthy mother is forced to raise a child by herself but does not successfully create a favorable environment for her child, the environment will be the influential factor in the outcome of the child's life. The problem is, we point to the mother as the cause of the unhealthy environment, which would otherwise be fair, but as it pertains to single-mother households, blame should be directed towards the absence of the father.

Now, while that wasn't a difficult conclusion to come to, some pretend they can't comprehend it by, instead, spreading the myth that it's the single mother who's causing criminals. They point to her character, instead of the circumstances she did not create outside of giving birth to a child. They quickly steer the conversation to whether or not she's married or if she did the responsible thing of making sure, beforehand, that she could financially supplement for an absentee father. You know, since that's apparently on the table these days. Yet people who are okay with that being on the table pretend to be outraged at the obstacles that arise in creating a healthy environment for a child to be raised in.

So it's not that single mothers are creating criminals, it's the obstacles presented by a father's absence in creating a healthy environment for a child that oftentimes results in a child going down the wrong path into a criminal life. Statistics don't tell you about the toll it takes on a parent to work overtime both in their career and in their role as a guardian when full-time obligations are a lot for anyone. Statistics won't show that a mother needs time to take care of herself, but the absence of a father leaves little to no room for that to happen. So, a woman who's suffocated by immense liability and responsibilities 24/7 will have difficulty doing that. What the statistics don't show, propaganda conveniently ignores so that the conversation can keep those who believe the unfair blame on single mothers is somehow factually based, appeased.

To relay this message in the past, I've used the analogy of two people who build a couch that has to be carried from their workshop into a bedroom. Now, if one builder leaves the other to carry this couch alone, the couch may end up chipped from being dropped by the builder who now has to carry the couch by himself. That doesn't mean that the builder who carried the couch by himself is bad at carrying furniture, it means that this task was never meant for one builder to begin with, and damage to the couch is a direct result of that. Ideally, we'd like that builder to have the bionic ability to carry the couch without a single mark on it, and although there are some who do, that should not become the new standard. The standard should remain that if you build a couch that must get carried afterwards, you should do your part to help carry it. But stating statistics about how most damaged couches are a result of builders left to carry furniture by themselves will continue to lower that standard while increasing the number of damaged couches in the process.

So, when I see a boy posing as a man spouting this rhetoric as a reason why he's not attracted to single mothers, I immediately know it's the truth that he's really repulsed by. The defense mechanism for his obtuseness is thinly veiled as scholarly understanding of the bigger problem to society that he, and his higher standard of morality, won't contribute to. I call B.S., and so should you, every time.

CHAPTER 8

"A woman can't raise a boy into a man."

Next time you go to a family cookout or your local salon or barbershop, just bring up a woman who's having difficulty raising her child, who so happens to be a male, by herself. I bet you my last paycheck that someone will chime in with, "Can't no woman raise a boy to be a man." I grew up hearing it in church, on TV, and everywhere else the conversation was being had, even as a young boy who was at the time being raised by a woman who was equipping me become a man.

For a while, I believed the false narrative, too. Not because I'd given it much thought as to whether or not it was actually true, but because when you don't think about it, it does make sense. Why would a woman be able to raise a boy to be a man if she's never been one? She doesn't have the parts a man has, so that must mean she wouldn't know how to teach someone how to function in life with those parts. But thankfully, one day, I did think about it. And the more I did, the more I mentally began to itch at the thought of how I ever let such an untruth fester in my subconscious when everything around me told me otherwise. Women raise boys into men every day, and it doesn't require their biological body parts to do so, but rather teaching them how to first be an adult and creating an environment that has the parts necessary to teach him firsthand what she can't about how to specifically be a man.

We think of "raising" or "teaching" a boy to be a man narrow-mindedly as if it can only be done by firsthand demonstration, but this is not true. Most icons in entertainment were not groomed by people who'd reached the level of success they did, but rather by people who knew enough to help them build a foundation of how to be great and created the environment where combined with the icon's natural God-given talent, that entertainer could live out their true greatness on a level no one had ever witnessed. As humans, we raise puppies into full-grown dogs without ever walking on four legs. How? We nurture them, give them a foundation, and what we can't personally show by example, we know that a healthy environment that allows them to walk on four legs and other things dogs do combined with their God-given instincts will take over the rest. The same is true for college professors who've never stepped foot into corporate America grooming students who go on to climb up corporate ladders, or basketball coaches like Phil Jackson who was a mediocre player at best, but coached Michael Jordan and Kobe Bryant to be the best in the world.

If a parent can raise their child into an adult, the child's natural instincts along with a healthy environment will supplement the rest. It's been done by single mothers all over the world who raised men like Bob Marley, LeBron James, and President Obama. Examples of women raised by single fathers include Aretha Franklin, Maya Rudolph, and Madonna. A woman doesn't have to walk in the exact same shoes her son does to teach him how to tie his. So long as the foundation she's set for him going into adulthood is strong, he will be fully capable of learning the rest.

Some confusion on this topic comes from different definitions of what it means to be a man, in which I think most have that wrong as well. By the time this book is released, this will be old news, but right now people are debating if a man is still a "real" man if he wears a romper. A man is not defined by what he wears but rather by what values he holds. He's defined by whether or not he keeps his word, handles his responsibilities, solves problems instead of looking for excuses, and helps those who can't help themselves. A woman can absolutely guide her son in the right direction so that he acquires these qualities and is able to apply them without compromising his natural instincts as a male.

A man can be gentle with a woman, yet still assertive in everyday life. His mother can teach that. A man can develop emotional discipline so that he's intentional about when and how he expresses his feelings while not being ashamed to have them. His mother can teach that, also. When it comes to being his own man as opposed to running behind his homeboys or using physical restraint when in a confrontation with a woman, his mother can steer him in the direction of positive male influences who've gone down that road before so that he acquires the practical steps needed to apply in those real-life situations. When a mother realizes that her son responds more to masculine energy when being disciplined, she can facilitate a "village" of men in his life that will give him the structure he needs so that it's transferrable in his behavior at home as well. This can be with deacons at the church, coaches from his sports teams, male teachers, etc.

Even with a father in the home, outside influences will help raise a child one way or the other. Look at how many people have gone astray from their parents' teachings due to being introduced to drugs or sucked into the street life. "Rebellious children" don't just sprout out of nowhere. They're shaped by something on the outside that's able to take control of something on the inside of them that overrides what their parents may have taught them. Vice versa, the same is true. Some children have come from toxic environments at home and gone on to create a life much better than the one they had as a child because of some outside influence that showed them they could. But if a mother chooses to leverage and manage the environment her child is in on a consistent basis growing up, the benefit can be exponential and shape him into what would sensibly be considered a real man.

The point is, we should've done away with the lie a long time ago that a woman can't raise a boy into a man. A mother can and historically has proven that she can do that by both directly pouring into him and becoming a catalyst for outside influences that will supplement where she falls short.

CHAPTER 9

"Single mothers are only looking for help."

When you go to a job interview, what's your main motivation? My guess is you're not going just because you enjoy the scenery on the way there, but rather with aspirations to earn a job. You're going for the job because you'd like to earn money to help you take care of your living expenses. When you go to a gym, why do you go? It's not so you can admire the interior decoration, but to work out, right? You want to work out so you can look and feel better about your body and health is my guess.

So it's safe to say that no matter what you do or what you invest yourself in, you're doing so because in some way that will provide you value, even if it's something charitable like giving back to the less fortunate. The value you get is reaffirmation that you are making the world a better place by contributing to the lives of others. You will gain greater happiness knowing that somebody's life was just made a little better because of your sacrifice.

But, why is a single mother expected to go into a situation in which she'll undoubtedly make sacrifices and provide value but receive nothing back? In a relationship where she's already stretched thin between herself and her child, she'll have to make time and allocate energy into loving a man, so shouldn't that man provide some type of value to her as well? If he only comes into the relationship to receive but provide no benefit to her, wouldn't that make him a user?

Let's remove the fact that she's a mother and speak strictly to her as a woman. If she remains in a relationship where there's no value to her while she's pouring value into her partner, she'll be used up until she has nothing left. No matter how much of her money, time, body, and support she has to give, if she doesn't receive the same in return, her well will eventually run dry. So by any logical standard, a man reasonably should expect to only come into a woman's life if he has some kind of value to provide to the woman he's undoubtedly expecting value from.

Those who wish to paint a single mother as desperate will call the value she expects to receive from a relationship "help" in an effort to shame her for requiring what she will bring to the table in other ways. It implies that she's deficient without a man's presence, and while it may be true for some, the only deficiency most single mothers are faced with are parental responsibilities, which makes complete sense as we've discussed several times throughout this book already. That doesn't mean she spends her life forcing that on random men.

I first saw this posted as someone's Facebook status where he stated how he can't stand that when a single mother gets in a relationship, she expects financial help and a stepfather. My initial thoughts were that even if she does have her own money, she's going to expect a man to still come in as an asset. She doesn't need any setbacks, so at minimum he needs to come in and already be self-sustained. But, if he has long-term intentions, he'll be part of if not the primary provider for the household. So, why would she not look forward to being able to rely on him later on in the relationship should she need a few dollars? My guess is, a man would want to be able to defer to her if he needed it too. Now, if that's all she wanted him for, her having a child wouldn't make any difference. There are single women with no children who will drain him for every dime he has as well as single women with several children who have enough money to support themselves, her children, and any man, too, if she felt like it. The object isn't to "watch out" for single moms, it's to watch out for users, period.

As far as being a stepfather, any good single mother is likely to be overly cautious with a new man meeting her child, not shoving them together. So out of the gate, if she is in a hurry to push her children on him, then that's not a woman he should want to settle down with, regardless. But, most women with children are more protective over them than they even are of themselves, so he likely won't have that issue. If things get serious, then yes, he would need to be ready to step into the role as a father, and nothing is negative about that nor should be surprising. A single mother is a full package, just like everyone else. If he was famous, then a woman would have to accept him and his fame. If he was in the military, then a woman would have to accept him and the fact that he may get deployed for months on end. Whatever it is, we're all some sort of full package, and he can't simply choose the parts he likes while leaving everything else. That's not how relationships work with anyone, children involved or not.

If a woman without children loves to travel, she's going to be looking for someone to travel with her. If that woman is an avid gym goer, chances are, she's going to be looking for someone who likes to work out. If a woman is a mother, yes, she'll be looking long term for a man who's ready to step into his role as a head of a family household. That doesn't mean she's desperate for anything, it just means she's not playing games so if a man plans on playing them, he needs to play with someone else.

CHAPTER 10

"She'll always belong to her baby daddy."

I f you see a cute puppy going down the street with a collar, what's your first thought? Probably something happy since puppies make everyone happy. Your second thought will likely be that the owner must be somewhere around looking for their lost pet. If you're a good Samaritan, you may even stop and look at the collar of the puppy to see if there's an address attached so that you can return it to its rightful owner. The problem is, everyone knows that women are not some kind of pet with the exception of a certain group of extremely vocal lowlifes who assert their foolish views about how they believe single mothers will always "belong" to their child's father.

After directing the question of what misconception is commonly associated with being a single mother to my Twitter followers, this is the one that disturbed me the most. Not because it's actually worse than the other generalizations, but because in no case is this ever true despite my general belief that there are exceptions to every rule. A woman under no circumstance ever "belongs" to her child's father.

Any man that even makes that claim is saying a lot about how lowly he thinks of women.

In order to belong to him, she had to first be property, figuratively speaking. This implies that a woman's competence doesn't exceed her emotions, and once she's emotionally tied to a man, those same strings will be there for him to pull indefinitely, and with that, she'll belong to him no matter what she chooses to do.

False. Women are not mindless robots incapable of making their own decisions, and men, irregardless of how much a woman loves us, are not mentally superior beings that by default possess control over our female counterparts. This bigoted thinking is the reason men think that our mere existence should expect the most from women in a relationship while giving her inconsistency and complacency.

Be it emotional ties or co-parenting responsibilities that come with a child, nothing serves as permanent glue between a man and a woman other than a commitment mutually made between the two of them. The implication of human ownership is disgusting and unfounded in reality. There are women who are begged by their child's father for romantic and sexual access to them and don't even entertain it, just like women without children who get begged by their exes for the same thing. There are even restraining orders, initiated by mothers against their child's father when he's shown that he's harmful to the well-being of the child. Some mothers will even go completely MIA on a father, which I don't agree with unless it's a life or death situation, but it does happen. So however you look at it, a woman "belonging" to her child's father at any point is ridiculous.

Will there always be a link between her and her procreator? Sure. Should that disqualify her as a worthy love interest? No. In the case that it does, it says that the only way for a woman to be desirable is to have no working nor platonic relationships with any male whatsoever, which screams "insecurity". Moreover, it also hints of a mindset that a woman is incapable of strictly platonic or working relationships with a man, which is rooted in the belief that women are inherently and mentally inferior so if a man wants something from her, he'll be able persuade her no matter what commitment she's made to another. That would make a link to any man a threat to her romantic relationship.

Of course, if two people share a child and are co-parenting, there will be a level communication necessary for that to be effective. That doesn't mean that emotional doors are still open; that means that a child's well-being is at stake so two adults must put emotions aside and handle their responsibility. Without having to co-parent, there are women who will hold emotional doors open for a man the same way there are women with no children who have the capacity to shut them and deadbolt them when it's all over. The common denominator is a woman who's mature enough to do the latter, but that woman deserves better than a man who needs that explained to him.

CHAPTER 11

"Single mothers are promiscuous."

A man can give a woman the most neighbor-waking, furniture-breaking, mind-blowing sex and still block her the next day because his wife got suspicious. A man can shell out a few dollars on a weekend trip out of town to give a prostitute a "ride" to the nearest gas station while making a pit stop on the way and not even remember what color lipstick she wore. A man will even get caught cheating, in the act, and immediately rationalize with his woman that it was "just sex" which is a not-so-nice way of saying, "Get over it because this simple act should be no reflection of me." The point is, sex is just a simple act unrelated to one's character...until a woman does it.

Anyone who passed through to the third grade knows that babies don't come from the baby fairy, so evidently if a woman has a child, there's a good chance she had sex to conceive it. But the thought that a woman's proof of at least one sexual encounter equates to a life of promiscuity is irrational at best, but more presumably another symptom of a belief that any amount of sex is too much sex for a woman, unless she's validated by marriage.

It's no different than when a man asks a woman's "body count", a.k.a. how many guys she's slept with before meeting him. In his mind, it's a measure of her character, the same character he would say is separate from his actions if he got caught sleeping with her best friend while she was at work. If a woman answers with anything other than "I've only been with two guys, and both of them were long-term relationships," she'll be ascribed the "hoe" asterisk by her name from that point forward.

So when a woman has a child and with a man she's currently not with, the assumption is that they weren't that serious to begin with, and therefore she's seen as the girl who gets around; at least this is the illogical progression of small minds. What makes more sense is that even though you're taking a risk of pregnancy any time you have sex, most times, children are conceived from unprotected sex. Unprotected sex is more common in relationships than it is random encounters since there's a level of trust and comfort established to even get to that point. So, if a woman has a child, there's a high likelihood that she wasn't just "getting around", she was in a relationship. But even if she was just getting around with as many unprotected partners as she could, she had help. And her getting around wasn't enough to stop whoever it was she got pregnant by, so what does that say for his standards and why are we not including him in the "promiscuous" conversation?

The problem is that we're inundated with images from the media of women who get knocked up and then end up pregnant in daytime television, box office movies, and more. While most children of single-parent households are born out of wedlock, there's no data supporting that a monogamous relationship wasn't in place at the time. But even without the numbers, you can look around and see that nothing supports the notion that women are just so easy to sleep with. If they were, men wouldn't have to come up with lies and tricks to do it. They'd just be up-front from the beginning, make clear that they don't want a relationship, and act accordingly. Men wouldn't try to buy expensive things, or lie and say they're single. If women were generally as easy and "promiscuous" to sleep with, men would walk into a bar, blink, and then take a woman home with them. Although we know that's not the case, promiscuity is marketed as a "woman" thing.

If that's not enough irony, consider this. Even men hold the belief that it's worse when a woman cheats in a relationship because it's perceived as more intentional when she has sex, as opposed to men who somehow have the inability to turn down sex because it's our nature to wildly sow our oats. That means we can accept that men are naturally and wildly wired to have sex without abandon, but don't see why promiscuity being largely associated with women makes no sense. This unevenly yoked burden carries over to single mothers and the perception that if they have even one child, it must mean they have less regard over their body than the unreasonably high standard a woman is supposed to have.

Most men that act as if promiscuity is exclusive to single mothers are really just hiding their insecurity of dealing with a woman who doesn't fit into the misogynistic expectation of "purity". It's a lot easier than just coming out and saying, "My boys are still as ignorant as I am and I don't want them to look at me as weak," when the weakest thing any man can do is be more concerned about what others will think than he is about the truth.

But wait, there's more. Because men aren't the only ones ascribing promiscuity to single mothers, so are other women who "didn't put myself in position to be a single mother," which is a phrase commonly used to promote themselves up the moral ladder of classism. The only way not to put yourself in position to be a single mother is to live and die a virgin because other than that, once you have sex, you're risking having a child, and if you get left high and dry afterwards, there's nothing you can do about it. It doesn't matter if you're married, just ask the divorce rate. Once a man is married to you, there's nothing you can do to keep him from divorcing you outside of putting a gun to his head, and even then, if he really wants to leave, he'd probably beg you to pull the trigger. It doesn't matter if you've been with the same guy for ten plus years or if you've only ever been with one man. If you've ever had sex, you've put yourself in the same position as any other single mother once was in, you just ended up with a different end result.

The separation is not in the amount of times you have sex or in your relationship status. While those things may influence one's chances, the lone deciding factor is in the presence of the man. If a woman sleeps around and has twenty children by twenty different men, she is only a single mother once any one of those men decides to forfeit their responsibilities as a father. You can't look down on a woman just because you got lucky and the condom didn't break, or the Plan B pill you took worked, or because you had enough money for the abortion, or because the father of your child hasn't left...yet. Good for you that things worked out how you wanted, but it's no different than two people who rob a bank where one gets caught and goes to jail while the other was able to escape. The person who escaped can't look down on the one who didn't, they just didn't get caught. So again, unless you live and intend to die as a virgin, you're just one man who has convinced you he's committed to you for life and runs away once the baby is born away from being in the exact same position as the women you judge.

CHAPTER 12

"They just want child support to spend it on themselves."

I remember a few years back, scrolling online and wasting more time than I care to admit, I came across a meme that read, "Child support should come on a card that only buys baby stuff." I didn't take it seriously, just figured it was meant to stir up conversation for the sake of getting likes and comments on a post. But the post didn't go away. It resurfaced over and over again from guys who were apparently using it to echo their sentiments about the money they paid to support their children.

After seeing it a few times, I decided to pay attention to the context around the posts from the men who shared it. Almost all of them held the belief that there was currently no structure to how their child support money was being spent, and was therefore being squandered on personal items for the mother instead of strictly "baby stuff".

But from talking to most mothers, the ones who do actually get child support, there are usually crumbs awarded by the courts. Other personal testimonies from actual mothers weren't far off and didn't line up with this alleged lavish lifestyle the disgruntled fathers were so concerned about.

It seems that the root cause of these fathers being upset is because they believe a single mother's income is the only one owed to their child, while anything a father chips in is bonus. That bonus, in their eyes, should come with strict limitations, although no limitation would truly satisfy them as they'd prefer to not pay child support at all. Well, one problem is, if a father actually does pay child support, most don't give nearly enough for any woman to splurge on. In fact, the payments are hardly even adequate for the tangible needs of a child that would classify as "baby stuff", not to mention things like rent for the roof over their head, gas to drive them to the hospital, electricity, etc. To that, I've heard some people say, "Well, she would have to pay those regardless." That is true, except she would not need the extra bedroom without the child. She would not need to turn on her gas stove to heat bottles or make food as often without the child. She would not need to turn on her TV, plug in nightlights, run the washing and drying machines, or run bath water without the child. So although it may seem minimal, a child does consume his or her share of utilities that should be accounted for. Furthermore, nobody lives expense-free, children included. When a parent sends their child off to a summer camp, even if the costs of all the rooms are accounted for, there would be a fee to cover the child's room that they're staying in. The parent can't say, "You'd have to pay for all of these rooms anyway. So, I shouldn't have to pay for my child to stay here." It's no different if a man's child is spending most of his or her time with the mother. The roof over that child's head should be accounted for and to the closest degree possible, split between the mother and father.

Another problem is that child support money is seen by many as an optional bonus or just "chipping in". No. There's a financial contribution expected from each parent regardless of who has custody per their ability to pay and the child's needs to be met. If a woman would be dead broke without child support, but has some discretionary income after child support to spend on herself, guess what? That's how it's supposed to be. A man's child support money is not simply to "help" the mom, it's to serve as whatever is his appropriate contribution to the household his child is in, regardless of how much the mom pays or how she spends her money after the child's needs are met. Again, if two people are to carry a couch, it's not one person's job to carry as much of the couch as possible, and for the other person to lend a finger to help carry whatever's lacking. Both people should grab a side and lift to the best of their ability without basing it on the other's contribution. As long as the couch is being properly lifted and both people are doing their part, the rest doesn't matter. As a matter of fact, a woman who's able to take care of herself after giving so much to her role as a mother would probably make for a better mother overall. If a man really loves his child and doesn't view him/her as just a financial responsibility, he should want the environment his child lives in to be pleasant, which is made possible when a woman is allowed to tend to herself, too. Why would a man be more comfortable with his child being raised by a woman who's constantly burned out and stressed out than he would be doing his part, knowing his child has everything they need and seeing the mother treating herself on top of that?

Another problem with this heightened concern about how "my money is being spent," is that with so much focus on the mother's lifestyle, they forget that this is all supposed to be about the child. Yes, there are some mothers who do not put their child first. But as for most, the child is well taken care of, and child support payments could never pay enough to cover everything, including the intangibles. For example, while it's nice to have help with food and daycare costs, there's not a price on a mother's contribution when the father's not there. There's not a price on explanations about why other children have their father present, but that child's father's concern is more about whether or not Mommy got a new purse instead of being as involved in the child's life in other ways. There's no price on explanations on why Daddy said he would come to watch them sing in the choir, but was hung-over from the night before or still laid up with his new girlfriend. There's no price on having to mentally be aware of what your child's doing and where they are at all times, while the father is able to spend most of his time the same way he did when he had no children. There's no price on the physical toll childbirth takes on a woman's body. Any man thinking that his contribution of a couple hundred dollars a month is excessive or even comparable to a mother's sacrifice is ignorant to the value a mother truly provides when she's otherwise raising the child primarily or solely on her own.

Child support does seek to at least financially mimic the father's presence, but it'd be more effective if it was inclusive of things a mother has to do as opposed to being put on a card strictly for "baby stuff". For instance, child support should lawfully require a father to have to find a babysitter for work or before he can go on any dates, since that's something mothers have to do. Twice a month it should put that responsibility solely on the father, and if he fails, fine him. Child support should also require the father to have to take days off from work when the child gets sick. It should automatically sound an alarm that wakes him up in the middle of the night every time the child wakes up and cries or is scared and wants to sleep with their mom. It may sound foolish, but nothing's more foolish than a father being able to get completely off the hook of parenthood outside of seeing a few dollars garnished from his check every month when a mother's contribution goes so much further than that.

Also, since plenty of voices on this topic have advocated for the mother's responsibility to "choose better men to lie down with," a fatherly credit score should also come with it. Although men with no children, yet, will still be able to fly under the radar, men with children they're already not taking care of will not be able to falsely paint this picture of the dad who can't get past their child's mom. A fatherly credit score would be the equalizer so there's no mistaking what kind of father they've been, or not been, for their child.

Just like an actual credit score, every time he misses a payment, PTA meeting, band rehearsal, soccer practice, disciplinary meeting at school, or school play, it should take away from his score. Every time he promises to come spend time with his child or tells them he'll call them but doesn't come through, it should knock that number down, too. If he even goes a week without calling or making any attempt to communicate with his child, that should count as much as a default on a loan. Since everyone places the onus on women to "choose better", it only makes sense that there's also added incentive and accountability to do better. So with that, any woman who meets him should be able to pull up his fatherly credit score the same way she can pull up any mug shots. If his credit score gets too low, he needs to have his cell phone repossessed so he can't keep fishing for more women to turn into single parents.

There's no reason he should be able to go out of town as he pleases with no responsibility to make sure his child is situated just because he's made his bi-weekly payment. Meanwhile the mother has to be on call 24/7 if she even thinks about getting her much-needed vacation. He shouldn't be able to enjoy full nights of rest while the mother is lucky to get an extra nap in the parking lot on her lunch break since she got woken up in the middle of the night. The list goes on, but there are simply too many excuses we need to stop accepting and hooks that we need to stop letting these sperm donors off of.

CHAPTER 13

"I don't even ask him for child support."

I'm the first to commend any parent who's getting it done on their own and doing a damn good job while they're at it. I've witnessed it firsthand, and I know that it's everything but easy. The financial, physical, emotional, and spiritual responsibilities to keep it all together are enough to break anyone, so those who stand firm get my hat off to them. Any parent who's making it happen by themselves despite not having the help they should have is a parent who put the survival of their child or children above what's right and wrong. But we have to be careful about bragging about not asking for child support.

The moment we turn not holding deadbeat fathers accountable on any level into an accolade for single moms, we inadvertently open the door for penalization of those who hold that father accountable because now, we're treating the "did it by herself" mom as the standard instead of the one who gets the assistance she deserves. For instance, it's great if, despite less than equal pay, a woman is able to go higher in a company than her male counterparts and earn more, but we must couple our applause with the appropriate focus on still fixing the wage gap. It's admirable if, despite racism, a black person can excel in a space dominated by white males, but we cannot let that turn into a blind eye to the fact that racism is still an issue that needs to be resolved.

So am I saying that we need to stop praising single mothers who find a way to make it happen without so much as asking the deadbeat father to do his part? No. In fact, I'd like to see more of it. But what would do the conversation justice is underscoring every mention of a stand-up woman who's doing it on her own with the fact that she should not have to when there's a fully capable father who chooses to sit down. There's no better bragging right about not asking a man for child support than in situations where you didn't have to ask him because he volunteered it.

CHAPTER 14

"Single mothers will never have time to date you."

In our society, I can appreciate the new trend of entrepreneurship becoming the new "cool". Even if some just say the term but don't actually apply themselves fully, at least it's becoming more relevant of a concept and has people attempting to create and build their own brands. Like any other massive shift in our culture, this heavily affects the dating scene, particularly as it pertains to what one would expect from a partner who's still in the building stages. Even if it's not entrepreneurship, most men will proudly boast that they're currently on their "grind", which means they're economically or career-focused, so any woman who plans on being in their life on a serious level has to be ready to fit into and be an asset to that.

Understandable. I think that no matter where you're at in life, in order to be moving forward, your priorities must be in order, and if your grind is your priority, the person you're with should expect to fit around it initially, until they can become an asset to it later and get more of you and your time. But when it comes to single mothers, many men seem to think differently.

Think of a woman with a child the same as a man with a grind. Her schedule is certainly going to be tighter than most, which would seem a bit inconvenient. But the same would be true if that man was already in a relationship and his wife had a child. Focus would shift, schedules would center around the new change, not just him anymore, and after some adjustments, time would be made to balance things out where the relationship gets the attention it deserves. No, it wouldn't be convenient in the beginning, but due to the woman he's with being worth it, he would still need to exercise patience to make it on the other side of this new change.

The difference with a single mother is, a new guy comes in at a different place on her priority list than if he was already with her beforehand. The commonality is in the space of time where he won't get as much of the woman as he wants initially, but if he's flexible and patient, he will earn a higher position on her priority list as time goes on and will soon get the attention he's accustomed to.

So it's not that she will never have time to date, it's that any man who wants to be a part of her life needs to, at first, be ready to fit into her available time. Even with a full schedule of being a primary or only parent, there will certainly be some time to date, just not time to waste. If she doesn't have time to date him at all, that likely means she's already recognized that he's there to waste her time, or she's just not that into him, in which I'd advise her not to waste his time either.

However, if the interest is mutual, and he knows to plan in advance and have backup plans, he'll stand a better chance of fitting into her life since she already has to do that for herself and the same would go for being in a relationship. The babysitter has to be reserved, as well as another on call just in case the first one backs out. She has to have an exercise routine she can do at home if she misses the gym. There's always a contingency plan because one can never predict everything that may happen when dealing with children. If he plans on dating her, then he has to take the proper steps to be a part of her time, and he has to be able to keep that appointment in order to be taken seriously going forward.

To a man who's used to dating women with no children and living without any of his own, it may seem like a hassle, which is fine if that's how he feels. Most parents would agree that they feel the same way at times, actually. But, when he runs across a career-driven woman, it's going to be no different. Her career will be her priority over him the same way a woman's child is, and he's going to have to get in where he fits in. He won't be able to just pop up whenever he wants to because she'll be busy. He won't be able to keep cancelling on her because she'll get tired of blocking space in her schedule for his inconsistency. He won't be staying up all night every night pillow talking with her because her work will call for occasional all-nighters or going to bed early so she can get up first thing in the morning.

A single mother can make time to date if she pleases, the same way a man or woman on their "grind" can, it just requires structure and kept commitments on the part of the person who wants to date them in the beginning to earn the most they have to offer down the road. If a man is looking for someone he can "Oh my bad, I forgot" to death, then no, a single mother won't have time for him. If he wants someone he can "I don't know, whatever you wanna do," to death, then no, a single mother won't have time for him either. With the time her responsibilities take up, a person who wants some of it will have to be willing to earn and be patient to have access to it, but the same is true for any woman's heart. If she's not worth that to him then he need not present himself as an option to her.

CHAPTER 15

"Single moms should stick to dating single dads."

There are few feelings in the world better than meeting someone you hope you like, and then realizing that you have so much more in common than what meets the eye. They like seafood, you like seafood. They like to travel, you like to travel. They have been through so much and are just tired of the games, and so are you. The more you have in common, the less you have to explain when the two of you are making memories together.

With that, it makes sense why a single mom would prefer to date a man who already has a child and vice versa. There's less to explain about dating someone who's also co-parenting, or why scheduling ahead of time is so important, or why meeting the child's other parent must happen once things get serious. I'm actually not in opposition to this, except for the notion that a man without children won't work with a single mother.

A man without children won't work if he has no plans of having a family. If he has no plans of having a family, he definitely won't have plans of stepping into an already established one. Some men and women prefer the idea of "starting fresh" so to speak, but the truth is, many are not ready to start at all, so they're timid about moving forward with someone whom they'd have no choice but to get ready if they want to be with them seriously. That's anyone's right to their preference and I'm not here to shame him or her for it. But a man without children who is ready to be a father although he's yet to have his own should be included in the type of man a single mother should "stick to" dating. In fact, whether a man has a child already or not, the only man who deserves consideration is one who's ready to not just be a father, but a good one.

If a man isn't taking care of his child, then no woman should be dating him. If a man doesn't want to ever be a father, then no woman who has family goals that include children should be dating him. Relationship goals must be mutual the same way family goals must be, and that should be the primary consideration for a woman with children. Does he want to not only be a father, but is he ready to be a good one? Of course, this is far enough down the road where things are serious enough for that next step, but the stigma that single mothers have no business dating men who have no children is rubbish.

Is it going to be more difficult to find a good man? Somewhat. But, in case you haven't noticed, it's not exactly a cakewalk for women without children either. However, as mentioned before, as a single mother, you would not simply be looking for just a "good" man, anyway. You're looking for the right man, the ready man. No matter if you have children or not, you would need the man who's ready, not just "good".

What that means is, if you're educated, well-traveled, have an expanded vocabulary and are health-conscious to the point you like to at least glance at the ingredients on a nutrition label before buying food products to consume, you're already out of the league of many "good" men. "Good" is commendable, but it doesn't guarantee a happy life because if he's not ready for what you come with, you two won't be compatible.

He'll get offended by your expanded vocabulary, intimidated by your education, think you're doing too much when you try to eat healthy, and will see traveling as so unnecessary that you won't be able to enjoy it with him. That's why "good" as a standard is better fit for just a friend, but not a life partner.

Some guys will even come along who are compatible on every level. They'll challenge you, inspire you, adore you and know how to show it, but because of emotional strings to their ex or toxic habits they've yet to put away, they're not currently ready for you. That's not an issue exclusive to just women with children, but women, period.

So as a mother, your "ready" package basically includes one who's prepared to be a good father, as well as compatible in other areas to be your partner. It's one more qualification he has to meet that he would have to meet regardless, if you ever wanted to have children at some point in the future. The benefit is knowing up front, who's not ready to be a father and having those men weed themselves out.

CHAPTER 16

"You need to be married before making children."

I get it. I get the statistics. I get the religion. I get the firsthand examples of what granddaddy and grandma had that you grew up wanting for yourself. I get all of it, and you're not wrong. Not only does being married before having children make sense from a practical standpoint, but it's also ideal. Marriage is generally regarded as the highest level of commitment, and while you can never guarantee anyone's full commitment to stay in your life, this would be as close as you could get. The benefits far outnumber any drawbacks as opposed to doing it otherwise, if the situation is healthy. The only problem is, few consider the fact that the latter part of the previous statement is the most important part of all, and without it, the marriage means nothing.

You see, just getting married before you make a child is only half of the story. The other half is that you would also need to stay married while the child is being raised, according to most people's logic. But positioning the child as an incentive to get or stay married may begin to compromise the real reason to be married in the first place, which is the person you're marrying is someone you can grow with and will help maximize the happiness you already have for the rest of your life. This only happens if the marriage is and remains healthy, and everything else, including a stable environment for the child, should be a byproduct of that. However, turning what would be an added incentive into the primary reason for doing something will be counter-productive to all involved.

If a woman is thinking solely or even primarily of the kids as the determinant for sticking out a marriage, and not of her own growth and emotional health, it's easy to put those things on the backburner until they no longer matter to neither her or her husband. She'll fall into the trap of just "doing it for the kids" when really she's dying inside be-cause the man she's with no longer loves her like he used to, and now he's acting on it, or because she's no longer loving herself and he's making it worse. Even though the child may not know all of the details, he or she will sense that energy is off, and will internalize it in whatever way makes most sense to them, which could have catastrophic affects on their esteem and self-identity for the long-term.

For example, Daddy comes home every day and shuts the door when he gets inside the bedroom with Mommy. Mommy comes out of the room an hour or two later wiping her eyes, barely able to make eye contact with her child and therefore keeps the conversation short when her baby boy is boasting of his golden star he earned that day in school. With a million things on her mind, she thinks nothing of it, not to mention it's taking every bit of her strength to simply keep from breaking down. At this point, her baby boy sees a mom that's no longer excited about his achievements and therefore internalizes that as a direct reflection of her love for him, or lack thereof. And when he internalizes that he's no longer loved, he may go looking for the closest thing to love, which would be a sense of belonging, oftentimes offered by a group. This group could be something productive like a sports team or band, or it can be something like a gang, cult, or bad crowd of peers who are headed down the wrong road in life. At such a young age, he doesn't have the wisdom to choose what's best for him, so he's likely to choose what appeals most or presents itself first, and fate takes it from there.

Another example is when Daddy barely comes home at all. He used to come home in the early evening to look over his baby girl's homework and express how impressed he was with her intelligence. But, now Daddy's just a sound of the front door closing after her bedtime and a forehead kiss before he retires to the guest room where he sleeps. Really, he's at such odds with Mommy that he hates even being in the same household as her, but Baby Girl interprets it as Daddy having more important things to do than hear about her homework, so maybe excelling in school isn't as important as she thought. Maybe it's only for young girls, and now that she's growing up, other things are more important, like being "fine" or looking "thick" as the boys at school tell her she is. When they tell her that, she gets a small semblance of the pride she used to feel when Daddy told her she was intelligent, and since that's the closest thing to it, she begins to indulge in it as the years go on. She conditions herself to see her value in her body as opposed to her mind, so that's what she uses to get what she wants, or rather supplements for what she really wants--love from Daddy. The sex at age twelve turns into an insatiable appetite for male touch until she's with one who does more than just touches, he hits her. But because she gets the attention that temporarily scratches the itch for Daddy's embrace, she doesn't know how to leave until she's already taken so much, she refuses to believe in love again.

These are just two examples of how a dysfunctional married household that would otherwise be best split up long before things get this toxic, unfortunately remain intact because the commitment for children begins to annul the commitment to growth and sustaining emotional health that would actually benefit the children. The destructive effects are not a reflection good or bad of parents, the married couple is, because most times, parents mean well and are doing the best they can under the circumstances. However, when the parents believe that the status of their relationship is more important than the status of the health of their relationship, the damage they're doing goes undetected for years, and in some cases, can't be undone by the time it's recognized.

So, being married is a well-advised preliminary step to having children, but without proper context, can cause harmful outcomes as it so often does. Therefore, the focus should shift beyond the paperwork that constitutes a legal union to the work between two partners to maintain an environment free of corruption and toxic daily habits that go unaddressed when the children are the only incentives for being married. A child is more likely to grow up feeling loved, confident, and complete even if split between two households to unmarried parents who are cordial than if raised under a roof with two married parents who hate each other.

CHAPTER 17

The Hypocrisy of "Harsh Truths" Single Mothers are Told

For every woman reading this book, I want you to think back to the first time you talked about your dream guy. Maybe you were talking to a bestie, your mom, or even in a conversation with a potential love interest indulging in some mental stimulation. While careful to mention that he didn't have to be perfect, you likely had every quality visualized down to the details of his teeth. His educational level, desire to see the world, height, muscular build, his taste in music, social consciousness, relationship with his mom were all a part of the package you felt like you deserved.

If it was one of your first times talking about this, then it was early on enough where you'd not already had these dreams shot down by the reality that it's a lot easier to describe those qualities than to find them. And, your description of these qualities almost inevitably were met with some version of the forewarning, "Your standards are too high" or "You can't have it all." Every woman has heard that at least once, no matter how realistic or not her standards are, and sometimes it may even be true. Most listening ears are well aware that the playing field isn't running rampant with all-stars. Whether it's strictly physical, or maybe mental, people won't let you even enjoy a hypothetical dream man anymore. They're quick to tell you to be humble and be open-minded to a guy who's shorter than you, doesn't have much money, doesn't speak how he feels, and maybe even cheats every now and again. Why? Because as some would say, "You gon' miss your blessing looking for perfection."

They spook you with the possibility of a life of loneliness and a house of cats, while everyone else has thriving families because they were able to look past a few imperfections, including those that would break your heart. There's no hesitation for them to pull your head out of the clouds where a man is designed and custom fit just for you. As a matter of fact, when in a relationship and the man you're with begins showing his true colors as someone you deserve better than, you're met with advice on hesitating to hold him accountable by those you consult with because "A man is going to be a man."

However, when it comes to women who bear a man's child who subsequently leaves her to raise the child on her own, everything changes. That's when you get told that you should've had much higher standards on the guys you entertained. You should've checked his family tree to make sure being faithful was in his genetics. You should've buffed your crystal ball so you could've chosen a man incapable of leaving the child he made with you. They'll package these condemnations about how much more steadfast you should've been with your standards in a box of what they call, "harsh truths".

And there lies the hypocrisy. It's "Lower your standards" when it comes to giving men a pass on their B.S., but then, "You shouldn't have lowered them" when it's time to judge you for a man who runs out on his responsibilities. I personally believe that you should always have your standards high, but I also know that your standards could be higher than the Eiffel Tower and it still won't give you psychic ability to forecast a deadbeat nor control over his action. So why is it that society thinks it can continue to disguise the B.S. they're trying to feed single mothers as a pill of "harsh truth" that's tough to swallow when it can't even get its story straight?

CHAPTER 18

For Guys Who Refuse to Raise Another Man's Child

I first came across this notion while scrolling on You-Tube. One of the self-proclaimed leaders of men demanded that men aim higher in life than to raise another man's child. As if it wasn't already going down-hill at that point, it plunged when he made the case that he shouldn't have to take on anyone else's responsibilities because that's her (the mother's) job. Yes, he actually said that, with legions of alleged men all in cahoots. However, that wasn't even the most laughable thing about the whole situation.

His videos reflected the same mindset you see in conversations today: A change in moral values depending on what was convenient at the moment without so much as two seconds to see how they conflict with each other. You see, while on one hand he preached that thou shalt not raise another man's child, he also had another video on tips on how to take any man's woman. That means that it's completely acceptable to have what another man has claimed so long as it pertains to a woman, not actual responsibilities.

But, my issue isn't with guys who won't raise another man's child, even if they will proudly try and take another man's blessing. My problem is with men who won't raise their own and those who pretend that the reason they don't want to raise another man's child is because there's something wrong with the woman. The "it's not my job" excuse is tired and doing a horrible job at disguising the reality that most men aren't ready for the work of being a parent, in which I'd respect a man more for just coming out and saying that instead. If we're really being honest, most men simply aren't ready for the work of being with a woman who's had any major life experiences, even when they are caused by the man himself.

For instance, many guys will cheat on a woman multiple times until her trust is shattered into dust, earn her forgiveness, then get mad when she asks him where he's going late at night. It's not because they thought the forgiveness came with forgetfulness. It's because they were convinced there was a way to bypass the work of fixing that trust issue they gave their woman before moving forward.

The same thing goes for a man who wants a woman to be physically and mentally the gold standard; no scars, no love handles, full lips, never nags, cooks like a Martha Stewart, and can turn into porn hub on his command. He wants all of that but also claims he doesn't know how to "communicate" when things get sticky in a relationship. He has ways that make it hard for his woman to love him but tells her constantly that "he's not perfect" instead of focusing on ways to improve for her sake. Why is that? Because it takes work to grow. It's no different than a guy being met with the challenge of one day being a parent.

The truth is, most guys really aren't ready for parenthood, and that's okay. Most women aren't either before they're forced to get ready. But there's an issue when a man can misdiagnose his inadequacy for parenthood and fragile ego with a character flaw for a woman who has a child, then stroke his ego with, "I ain't raising another man's child" because in many ways he's still a child himself.

CHAPTER 19

Why Single Mothers are for Grown Men

In the beginning of this book, I mentioned how the video that sobered me from the illusion of a rationally thinking society when it came to the subject of single mothers, was titled, *Single Mothers are for Grown Men Only*. I clearly articulated my points one by one, starting with the fact that women with children won't have the same discretionary time available for a man to grow out of things that a woman without children may have. There's no better or worse between the two, it's simply a matter of scarcity, in which time to be wasted won't be as abundant for a woman who barely has enough time to allocate to things that are necessary. A woman without children may be able to suffer a few years of growing pains for a man who may eventually get his act together, but a woman with children has too much to lose in waiting out that process. If she entertains a man who likes to go ghost to make her chase him, that's a future ghost of a father figure which will multiply the damage caused by the first one on children who may or may not recover from it in the long-term. If she's fortunate to have a father she's co-parenting with and entertains a man who, due to his insecurities, doesn't feel comfortable with her having any contact with former romantic partners, his jealousy could disrupt the relationship between the child and his or her father, or worse, cause the child to choose sides between the mother and the father.

A childless woman may get caught up in a life of crime with a man, go to jail for a few years, learn from those mistakes, and start a new life. If a mother goes to jail, she could have her children taken from her forever, even if she gets her act together afterwards. She'd miss moments and possibly years that she'll never get back. Her children may bounce across foster homes and internalize the feeling of being out of place, resulting in low self-esteem or vain efforts to identify with groups that ill-serve their future. There are too many immediate drawbacks that can leave a trail of irreversible scars on children who will start a cycle of pain and dysfunction for generations to come when a mother swims in the same dating pool as a woman without children. So, when I say single mothers are for grown men, it's not some feel-good mantra to help mitigate the undue shame a woman feels for no longer being first choice for some bachelors, it's a truth that women at any stage of life would be wise to take heed of.

With the consequences more severe for almost every mis-step, the stakes are risen for those who want to join the journey of a mother as her life partner. The stakes, or standards, men will have to come prepared to meet will be measured by their maturity. As much as single mothers are for grown men, more importantly, they are not for the mentally immature, or what I call grown boys. Grown boys are unclear about their intentions with a woman. A single mother requires structure. The evaluation stage of a man will only last so long for a mother because time with him will always mean time without her children. After a while, the time spent with her will evolve into time spent with the children, and if he has yet to make up his mind about what he wants from a future with her, then the relationship will be unstable and so will be plans for moving forward. Grown boys spend their time whimsically on whatever can grab their attention, be it video games, hanging out all night, or playing the field with other women. Single mothers will be using precious time that's not available at a moment's notice to get to know a potential partner, so understanding the importance of priorities and planning will be critical for effective dating. If she's constantly getting texts about "Wyd?" as a segue into an invitation to spend time when she's already committed to ten different things she's yet to get to on her to-do list, there will never actually be time to spend.

Grown boys have toxic ways of communicating, oftentimes resulting to yelling or even violence to get their point across. If a single mother tolerates such disrespect or abuse, it will be normalized in the eyes of her children who will grow up to communicate the same way. Their relationships will continue to fail no matter how compatible their partners are, and they may harm their children in the same way they were damaged as children. Grown boys play mind games to absolve themselves of any wrong, no matter what the situation, and will turn the tables so that the woman they're with feels like she's to blame. Single mothers are already teaching children about accountability for their actions and won't be able to do so if they give their partners passes for doing the exact opposite. Children are sponges of both words and actions and will have a hard time acting out the opposite of what they witness on the regular. Grown boys run out the moment things get shaky, breaking up to make up later after they've indulged in a sexual "breather". Single mothers will need a man who values commitment more than convenience, the same way being a parent requires you to stick things out, even when they're uncomfortable. If a woman can't respect inconsistency, how can a child? If a child can't respect a man, how can that man raise him or her?

Grown boys have internalized and will defend the generalizations previously mentioned throughout the earlier chapters of this book and will use them as excuses to mentally remain a child, or as covers for their desire to feel superior to someone since their actions rightfully place them at the bottom of the dating barrel. Their subconscious hides them from their own guilt by throwing single mothers under the bus every chance they get, and that's why single mothers will be best served reserving themselves for men who are already grown, as opposed to trying to develop the mentality of those boys so that they grow up.

Grown women, or more specifically, single mothers are for grown men. Grown boys or immature men really aren't for anyone at all, but they can at least be tolerated by women who have less to lose, especially those who are willing to be patient and endure the scars sure to come from the growth he's yet to experience. An immature woman will only enable the ways he's still mentally a child, causing them both to eventually self-destruct or live in dysfunction unless one of them smartens up, first and leaves or they both have an epiphany that they can do better to and for each other. You'll see this scenario reflected in many romance movies and novels, although it rarely happens in real life, but it is possible. A naïve woman will be brainwashed into thinking he's a grown man, and define love as well as her worth by the experiences she has with him. Whether their relationship lasts or not, she'll always hold him as the standard, and any man who exceeds that will be "too good to be true" because she's convinced herself she only deserves the treatment she's used to. But a grown woman and an immature man, or vice versa, will simply result in time and energy wasted, something single mothers can't afford.

CHAPTER 20

The REAL "Harsh Truth" About Single Motherhood

I'm not the biggest fan of kicking a dead horse. You've heard it before, and a lot of it has been true for some. You can't make a man stay by simply having his baby. You can't expect sympathy for being a mom before you're ready. Government assistance is no guarantee. Get another job and make it happen. Take him to court if it's that bad. Etc.

But the real harsh truth is that as a single mother, even though you don't deserve nearly as much blame as you get, you can handle it. No, it feels like you can't at times, and I'm sure you'd rather not. I know it's difficult to go from a normal life as a normal woman to being treated as if problems all start with you. I get that you've never known what a single mother has gone through until you're going through it and need help to get through it. The harsh truth is that until this world smartens up, it's going to remain dumb and cold. It's going to give you undue criticism and under-appreciation even though being overworked becomes your way of life.

If you haven't learned this yet, you can't always expect the best from someone just because you see it in them. You may have to pay double for your mistakes when someone else runs out on their bill. The mistake isn't the child you make, but rather the time and situation in which you bring them into the world, and you'll be left with the task to communicate that to your child as well as many other things

Another harsh truth is that when you don't want to be strong anymore, you'll be made to. Why? Because it's inspiring someone who is looking at you even when their eyes aren't on you. It's teaching them how to respond to times when life proves just how unfair it can get. It's showing them what kind of strength and resilience is inside of them before they get into a situation that calls for it to be put to the test. More importantly, it's a firsthand learning lesson before they have to learn it the hard way. So, even if they do end up in the same situation, they'll be able to respond positively, instead of imploding like the pressure is capable of making anyone do.

Most importantly, in order to display that strength, you have to use the strength you have wisely. Every battle is not yours to fight. This war on single mothers started long before you and will go on long after you. If you try to fight it, it will engulf you. You have to accept that people's ignorance is not your burden. When you leave them to carry it themselves, you'll be able to pick yourself up. You'll be able to hold your own head higher, and the higher you hold your head, the more clear the bigger picture becomes that while it may not have been your plan, your story is unfolding exactly as it was meant to and you will come out in the end as the victor.

CHAPTER 21

Single Mother "To Not Do" List

Whether you are a single mother or not, who knows what the future holds for you? You may one day find yourself in a situation where the man you've carried children for turns out not to be who you thought, or some life-changing event happens that actually transforms him into someone else you can no longer be with. Or even if you're a man, your daughter may one day find herself in a situation where she's doing it on her own, or maybe a sister, cousin, or whoever. No matter what the situation, among the laundry list of things society will bombard them with about what they shouldn't have done, there are actually some things that no single mother should do:

1. Do not entertain anyone just to say you have someone. That includes the man you procreated as well as probable prospects who show themselves but haven't proven themselves yet. Easier said than done, I know. But now, more than ever, picking a man as a placeholder or by default is dangerous.

Besides the obvious, that he could be a serial killer that

wipes out you and your family, you may forget that the time you're investing in him does cause feelings to take root. As much as you may be aware that he's not the one and you're just "doing it for the kids", your heart won't make that distinction if you're putting time and energy into him to keep him around. Feelings are similar to love; they make us all dumb. They take a seat at the decision-making table of your actions, sometimes several seats until they represent the majority, and will cause you to be vulnerable with someone you shouldn't have gone anywhere near to begin with. The wrong man overstaying his welcome in your life will hold you back, beat you down, or both; and it'll only hurt worse knowing that you knew better all along but didn't do better.

Not only can it be a huge blow to you as a mother, but it can also block the place your soulmate would fit in to your life. You may over occupy yourself prematurely due to the pressure of being a mom and doing it alone while missing out on what would be your partner for life because you're involved with a temporary fix. "Just stay single" is already an unsavory recommendation, and when you add children into the mix, it only gets more sour, but it's practical. You'll be alone, it'll be hard, but you won't have anyone else wasting your time. It'll get lonely every now and then, sometimes for long periods, but you won't be overextending yourself just to be under-loved by someone who doesn't deserve you. It's nice to have a man around, but sometimes, no man is better than just any man.

2. Do not see yourself through the limited scope of society. Yes, another one that's easier said than done, but so critical in the quality of not only your own life, but also the life of your child. At some point, we choose to own or discard the messages we receive, both externally and internally, and what we own determines how we treat everyone around us as well as ourselves.

For instance, there's no amount of "pretty" that can convince a girl who believes she's hideous to walk with her head up and feel beautiful. There's no amount of talent that convinces a guy who believes he's worthless to pursue his dreams. And there's no amount of praise that convinces a single mother who's accepted the lie that she's any less of a woman than the next one that she should live out her life to the fullest and look forward to the best the world has to offer. However, not doing so will trickle from her own day-to-day mood to the mood of her child.

As mentioned before, one of the biggest determining factors of a household of whether or not the child is given a proper chance in life is not whether or not there's a relationship present, but whether or not the one or ones leading the household are in a healthy state of mind. Even though a woman may have perfected the smile and "I'm fine" responses to those who inquire, accepting any negative notions exclusive to single mothers is anything but healthy. It will cause her to accept less than what she would if she looked at herself, and saw her true value because we accept from others only what we see in ourselves.

It's similar to when a mother is disciplining her child and she gets talked back to, so she asserts that she is the adult, not the child. In that situation, the mother sees herself and rightfully recognizes that she's an adult, and therefore will not tolerate being treated or talked down to as if she's anything less. The same goes for a single mother who constantly hears slander, but discards it all as the rubbish it is, and instead reaffirms her own worth and owns that. The moment anyone comes to her and tries to treat her as something less, she will reject it, which will protect her peace, happiness, and energy from all leeches.

When you see a single mom or anyone for that matter, remaining in toxic relationships, dead-end jobs, or unhealthy environments, it's never a matter of "just doing what I got to do", even though that's the common reasoning. It's because they only see themselves as being good enough for those circumstances, and even if they've entertained the thought they maybe they could do better, it's not strong enough to propel them into action.

This is why we have to be careful about the messages we accept as truth. In fact, we have to be careful about the messages we even entertain and expose ourselves to, regardless of what decision we make to accept or reject it. When we're not, our subconscious may override our decision and accept it for us. It happens gradually, but when it does, it's difficult to undo, and may take so much time that the damage incurred in the meantime is permanent. Whether it's videos you watch online, group talks you sit in on, music, movies, or people in your circle, you have to be proactive about protecting your subconscious from negative messages that can pollute your self image.

3. Do not "debate" with imbecils.

It's going to be tempting, being that there are so many around. They'll pop up left and right, volunteering garbage that nobody asked for the moment "single mother" is mentioned, but whatever you do, don't debate with them. You'll be better off pouring water into a bottomless cup or telling a STOP sign to GO.

It's not because a debate couldn't be constructive, it's more so about who it's with, which ultimately determines where it will go; nowhere fast. Imbecils aren't just people who are misunderstood, they're those who are committed to misunderstanding. They're people who delight in seeing you put in the effort to correct them and will continue to delight the longer you try, which serves as an incentive to keep you going in circles. Imbecils often go the extra mile and create content on public platforms to help them spread their garbage like Twitter, YouTube, and Facebook. I've seen entire groups created just for the sole purpose of baiting anyone with a firm belief in the truth and the optimism needed to take them and their ignorance on head first. Whatever you do, don't feed into them.

Even when you corner an imbecil into a debate, they'll change the subject, insult you or whatever will frustrate you enough to keep the conversation going. You may think that because you're speaking in front of impressionable minds that a side of truth would be helpful, but it's still too slippery of a slope to get caught up on. You're likely to either get caught up addressing so many fallacies that you're in a web before you know it or you won't cover enough ground to have the upper hand in the eyes of those you wanted to provide your perspective to.

Choose those you have these conversations with wisely. They need to be worthy of not only your time and attention, but also of your subconscious that you'll expose to them by conversing with them, as mentioned previously. The person you dialogue with about single motherhood should go through a screening that starts with a track record that proves their heart is in the right place, even if they're off the mark. If it's not, you may not be debating with an imbecil, but rather a very intelligent and manipulative man or woman who's intentionally toying with a subject you hold near and dear. If you're not sure, it's best to leave it alone and let them go on about their day. The topic deserves progressive conversation, not circular vehicles of more stereotypes to be reinforced.

But if their heart is in the right place and they have the wherewithal to comprehend your experience as well as the information you have based on experiences of others, conversations can be extremely beneficial. Mental doors can be opened for those unknowingly ignorant to the truth. Hearts can be opened that never realized they were closed. The proper discourse at the right time is the first step to undoing decades of misperceptions, but with the wrong people, it can simply be a waste of your time.

CHAPTER 22

How to Know Who You're Dealing With

I remember as a teenager, back when you couldn't use the Internet if someone was on the phone and MySpace was the hottest social media site in the world, there was an "About Me" section that asked just about every surface-level question you can think of such as a person's favorite color, height, shoe size, grade level, etc. This gave the illusion that you could get to know someone first, before connecting with them personally.

Of course, we look back on that and realize it's ridiculous, but many of us aren't sure what the actual next step should be. No, his favorite color won't give you a glimpse into the longevity he's looking for, but what does? What is it that tells you his true intentions, or despite his intentions, his capabilities to fulfill you? Well, there's no guaranteed way to know being that we're all complicated, evolving, and masters of mixed signals, and anyone who tells you that there is, is lying. However, there are some things that are more likely to give you an accurate assessment than MySpace's metrics.

One question that would get you a closer look at who he is would be, what experiences can he speak on that's shaped how he views the world today? This is one of those things you can cover in the very first conversation you have with him, and although these things can be rehearsed, many liars and manipulators these days are lazy. If you make them work hard enough to fabricate an answer for a question like this, they'd rather take their chances with someone a little less probing. This is the part where he should be able to speak on things he's done wrong as well as things that have given him gratification that he's doubled down on since he discovered it. In this, you can listen to whether or not his experiences align with someone who's ready for a family.

If his experiences are that of a young, wild, and free bachelor that he's just now getting a chance to explore since he was in a committed relationship for so long, then that doesn't mean he's a bad guy, but he's probably not the one for you. If he's never known real love, or even had a reason to give it serious thought, so now he's in a "Whatever happens, happens" space in his life, that's also likely not the man for you. However, if he's tired being a player and got burned, and currently protecting his space and reserving it for someone he can grow with as well as willing to take the time needed in order to nurture that for the long haul, he's worth further consideration.

Secondly, one of the most invaluable things you can do before becoming completely vulnerable with a man is observing him in various moods and situations. If the sailing is smooth when you meet him, that's great, but tread carefully. Anyone can be Mr. right when things are easy. But how does he handle being told, "No?" How does he handle financial setbacks? Does he go to any length to get money, including illegal activity and manipulation, or does he have too much integrity to stoop that low. Does he immediately go into a depression that you'd be responsible for getting him out of, or does he just need a minute to process the situation before he makes a plan and executes?

When he's hurt by something someone close to him has done, what's his reaction to that? Does he justify any level of revenge or is he in a place where he asserts himself as the bigger person? Does he tell all of their personal business because they "deserve it" or does he simply move on and cut them out of his life? Although getting to know any man is never a risk-free process, you can't be quite as bold with the risks you take with so much on the line. Maybe you can up and leave a situation the moment things look scary when you're by yourself, but once a child is tied up into your relationship, you'll have to navigate through explanations, child custody laws, and other strings attached, particularly if you get married to him. It may take some time, but if you have only seen a man in good times, then you haven't really seen him at all.

This point is worth emphasizing because the man who comes into your life is no longer applying for an entry-level job. That was in high school. Minimum requirements and availability was just fine, back then. Looking good, smelling good, and remembering to slide the dinner tab his way was good enough back then. But now, you're not only an adult, but you have a dependent. The man coming into your life is applying for a much more serious position that's going to require more, therefore you must do more in order to validate that he has the minimum requirements. If he doesn't, it doesn't mean that he won't make a good husband one day, it just means he's not the future husband for you. You're at a point in your life when you need a man readymade, not assembly-required.

Often, we're reminded that you can't "fix" a man. That means if he comes in with any level of dysfunction, bad habits, or unhealed wounds that pre-exist you, it's not your responsibility to try and fix it. Although true, the same goes for a man without anything necessarily wrong with him, he's just behind the learning curve when it comes to being a relationship partner for you.

Within reason, you'd expect to have to grow into one another. He would have to learn your likes and dislikes the same way you'd have to learn his. You both have some area to grow to be a better relationship partner, period. But, when a man comes and needs, not just a few tweaks, but assembly from scratch, then he's simply under qualified for the job. Imagine someone coming to work the cash register at a restaurant, but they can't even count to ten. While any supervisor would understand that there's a learning curve for their particular system, there are some basics that you need to come equipped with in the very beginning.

So as for a relationship, if he doesn't know that he shouldn't curse around your child, that he has to plan in advance to spend time just out of respect, that he has to have a financial plan or at least working on a savings stash in case of emergencies, that you won't just "see what happens" with the relationship status, or that you already have a child to raise and won't be raising him, too; he's simply not qualified. Even as amazing as he may be and all the parts to be amazing for you, the assembly is his responsibility, and walking away once it's evident that it's not done is your responsibility.

CHAPTER 23

Please Be Selfish

As a single mother, or single woman in general, you can prepare for and be optimistic in hopes of coming across a grown man, but chances are, there will be a process before that finally becomes a reality. Even when you do meet a grown man, that doesn't mean that he's going to be right or that it'll be the right time in his life for what you're looking for. So, coming to terms with that reality is no longer just a nice option, it's a mandate for those who don't intend to wait for a man to serve them happiness in a tomorrow that's not promised.

Yes, that means being happy, even in your singleness, which will in turn, give you your leverage to get exactly what you want from a relationship. The moment fear, impatience, or frustration becomes your primary emotion, you're at the mercy of the next remotely close love interest to give you just anything that you'll convince yourself is something special.

No, it's not fun sleeping alone, waking up alone, or looking at your phone and seeing no new texts from anybody who's curious about your day. But it's downright depressing if that's all you focus on. The only reason you'd focus solely on being alone is if your idea of how life should be is with someone, but that's not always the case. Even for married couples, at some point, they needed to be single. Some need to be single now, but that's a different story.

But as a woman, mother or not, there are times in your adult life when you'll need to be single. Either you're not fully prepared for what's for you, or what's for you isn't fully prepared for you. The right things still must come together at the right times in order to be right. So instead of trying to align the stars to assuage your boredom or jumping at the very first sign of hope, it's better to discipline your focus on things that will change your quality of life immediately without waiting for Mr. Right to fall into your lap.

For one of the few times in your life, you have room to be selfish. Not selfish in a sense of being self-serving and not caring about other people's feelings, but rather selfish as in taking care of you properly. While your child will always come first, even before yourself, it's healthy to have spaces you can go to just work on and tend to you with no obligation to anyone else. Being single permits that space to be easier to reach, especially without having to explain when or why you need to go there.

That doesn't mean that when you get into a relationship, you stop taking care of you first. It just makes it easier to incorporate if you've already established that as a part of your life as opposed to overextending yourself first and then trying to figure out what it is you're missing while simultaneously trying to love everyone else.

CHAPTER 24

So, What Now?

No matter how much logic, reasoning, or inter-vening efforts are deployed upon you as a single mom, I'm betting that if there ever was, then there still is a small residue of guilt lingering on your sub-conscious. The same guilt that women have when they're dealt a broken heart from a guy they should've "known better" than to fall in love with. The same guilt you feel from that one friend who crossed you that you should've "known better" than to trust. Chances are, you feel like you should've "known better" than to lie down with this man who eventually left. Along with that guilt, there's usu-ally a fear that tags along about how a man will perceive you now. Follow that with experiences of running into so many mental adolescents posing as grown men who only have childish intentions and that fear can turn into dwin-dling hope that the true love you've always wanted won't choose you in this lifetime.

At this point, it'd be a bit of an overkill to state why those thoughts are inaccurate, but if you're looking for some-thing you can do to affect your situation going forward, you do have options. First, forgive yourself and let go of that guilt. You didn't know better, and nobody did before they learned. The rest of us just got lucky and didn't have to learn the hard way. Secondly, screw the negativity circulating outside because it will not be going away anytime soon. This book and many more will be written over the coming decades, and it still won't be enough to change everyone, so you can count on encountering a level of ignorance until the day you die. So, until you can look yourself in the mirror and acknowledge that your opinion matters most and their opinions matter none, you'll never find or sustain true happiness. Those with the opinions of you have not, nor do they care to do their homework on, exactly what led to your situation. They don't care to know what all you've done to make the best of it. They won't dare make any effort to hold the absentee father accountable or supplement the money that he's not paying. The outside chatter is coming from people who will not help you and wouldn't even if they could. One of the most beneficial things you can do is to recognize that and act accordingly by regarding their misperceptions as the bullshit it is and keep your head high.

The last thing you can do is to guard your heart and your body like never before. While you want to be open to love, you also want to make those who come into your life meet a higher standard to prove that's exactly what they're bringing. Not dysfunction, fun for a night, "Let's just see what happens", expectations of being fixed, or excuses about why you should wait for them to grow up into a man who's ready for the role they knew they'd have to be stepping into from the beginning. They should be bringing the kind of love that keeps them too honest to string you along with no long-term intentions, the love that would never allow them to see you struggling with anything without them doing whatever they can to help you, and the kind of love that would have them keep their distance if they're not ready for every bit of you instead of just bits and pieces.

Although your guard or lack thereof isn't the problem, nor does how guarded you are ever make you responsible for a man who runs out on his obligations, the reality is, the world is broken, but it's the only one we have. Until it's no longer broken, the most practical thing you can do is to handle it with caution. Require more to get close to you. The one who's bringing more won't be turned off. Require a longer period of time to receive the best from you. Those in it for the long haul won't be impatient. While absolutely nothing can guarantee any result, you can rest peacefully knowing that you acted on the experiences you've had the best way anyone could. You did adjust the wiser you got. You took better care of yourself and invested less in the outside ignorance of what's going on inside. With that, your guilt will have no justifiable reason to remain with you, and the burden of a broken world will no longer be on your shoulders to carry consciously, or subconsciously. Even with scars of a broken heart, you'll no longer be shackled by guilt for a transgression you didn't commit. Keeping yourself shackled to that guilt is a form of torture, and you can't torture yourself and properly love yourself, nor can you properly love anyone else if you don't love yourself. So, if you take anything away from this book, please remember this one thing; you owe your love to yourself first. If you can always remember that, a grown man will have no problem recognizing and loving you just as much as you do.

THE END

CPSIA information can be obtained
at www.ICGtesting.com
Printed in the USA
FFHW020126120219
50510158-55771FF